This Is What I Want to Be

Astronaut

Heather Miller

Heinemann Library
Chicago, Illinois

Customer Service 888-454-2279
Visit our website at www.heinemannlibrary.com

Designed by Sue Emerson, Heinemann Library
Printed and bound in the United States by Lake Book Manufacturing, Inc.

07 06 05 04
10 9 8 7 6 5 4 3

Library of Congress Cataloging-in-Publication Data
Miller, Heather.
    Astronaut / Heather Miller.
        p. cm. — (This is what I want to be)
Includes index.
Summary: An introduction to the educational background, equipment,
clothing, and various duties of an astronaut.
    ISBN: 1-4034-0364-3 (HC), 1-4034-0586-7 (Pbk.)
    1. Astronautics—Vocational guidance—Juvenile literature. 2. Astronauts—Juvenile literature.
    [1. Astronautics. 2. Astronauts. 3. Occupations.] I. Title.
    TL850.M55 2002
    629.45'0023—dc21

                                   2001008131

Acknowledgments
The author and publishers are grateful to the following for permission to reproduce copyright material:
p. 4 Frank Whitney/Brand X Pictures; p. 5 Corbis; pp. 6, 9, 10, 11, 13L, 14, 15, 16 NASA; pp. 7, 8, 17T, 18, 19B NASA/ Roger Ressmeyer/Corbis; p. 12 Bruce Coleman Inc.; p. 13R Science Photo Library/Photo Researchers, Inc.; pp. 17B, 21 NASA/Science Visuals Unlimited; p. 19T NASA/Corbis; p. 20 Robert Llewellyn/Pictor; p. 23 (row 1, L-R) NASA, Corbis, Stockbyte/PictureQuest; p. 23 (row 2, L-R) Corbis, NASA, NASA; p. 23 (row 3, L-R) NASA, Bruce Coleman Inc., NASA/ Roger Ressmeyer/Corbis; p. 23 (row 4, L-R) NASA/Roger Ressmeyer/Corbis, Corbis, NASA

Cover photograph by Science Photo Library/Photo Researchers, Inc.
Photo research by Scott Braut

Special thanks to our advisory panel for their help in the preparation of this book:
Eileen Day, Preschool Teacher
Chicago, IL

Ellen Dolmetsch, MLS
Wilmington, DE

Kathleen Gilbert,
Second Grade Teacher
Austin, TX

Sandra Gilbert,
Library Media Specialist
Houston, TX

Angela Leeper,
Educational Consultant
North Carolina Department
of Public Instruction
Raleigh, NC

Pam McDonald, Reading Teacher
Winter Springs, FL

Melinda Murphy,
Library Media Specialist
Houston, TX

We would also like to thank Kacy Kossum, Newsroom Coordinator at the Johnson Space Center, for her review of this book.

Some words are shown in bold, **like this.**
You can find them in the picture glossary on page 23.

Contents

What Do Astronauts Do?

Astronauts study space.

They learn about stars and **planets**.

Astronauts take pictures of the **earth**.

They sometimes fix broken **satellites**.

What Is an Astronaut's Day Like?

Astronauts exercise in space.

They run on a **treadmill**.

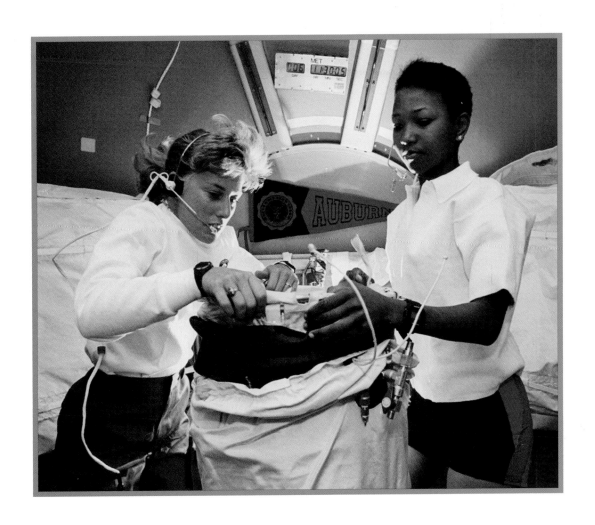

Astronauts keep the **space shuttle** clean.

They put everything away.

What Do Astronauts Wear?

helmet

air tank

gloves

boots

Astronauts wear **space suits.**

Space suits help astronauts breathe in space.

Astronauts put on space suits to work outside the **space shuttle**.

They take off the space suits when they are inside.

What Tools Do Astronauts Use?

robotic arm

Astronauts use **robotic arms.**

They can move heavy things.

jet pack

Astronauts sometimes wear **jet packs.**

Jet packs help astronauts move around in space.

Where Do Astronauts Work?

rocket

space shuttle

Some astronauts work in a **space shuttle**.

A **rocket** lifts the space shuttle into space.

space station

Astronauts can live and work on **space stations.**

Sometimes, astronauts work outside the space station.

Do Astronauts Work in Other Places?

Not all astronauts travel to space.

Some astronauts stay on **Earth**.

They work in the **control room.**

They help guide the astronauts who are in space.

When Do Astronauts Work?

Astronauts can stay in space for many days.

They work for many hours at a time.

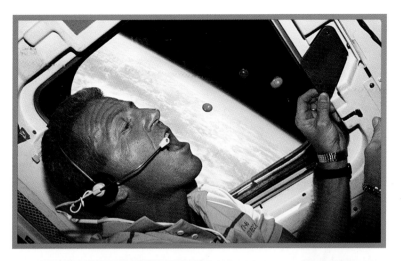

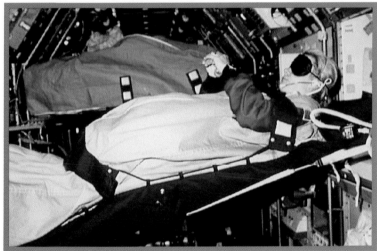

They eat in space.

They also sleep in space.

What Kinds of Astronauts Are There?

There are many types of astronauts.

Pilot astronauts fly the **space shuttle**.

Some astronauts set up special tests.

Others make sure the space shuttle is working well.

How Do People Become Astronauts?

People go to college to become astronauts.

They study science and math.

They train at a space center.

They practice with tools they will use in space.

Quiz

Can you remember what these things are called?

Look for the answers on page 24.

Picture Glossary

control room
page 15

planet
page 4

space shuttle
pages 7, 9, 12, 18, 19

Earth
pages 5, 14

robotic arm
page 10

space station
page 13

jet pack
page 11

rocket
page 12

space suit
pages 8, 9

pilot
page 18

satellite
page 5

treadmill
page 6

Note to Parents and Teachers

Reading for information is an important part of a child's literacy development. Learning begins with a question about something. Help children think of themselves as investigators and researchers by encouraging their questions about the world around them. Each chapter in this book begins with a question. Read the question together. Look at the pictures. Talk about what you think the answer might be. Then read the text to find out if your predictions were correct. Think of other questions you could ask about the topic, and discuss where you might find the answers. Assist children in using the picture glossary and the index to practice new vocabulary and research skills.

Index

Answers to quiz on page 22

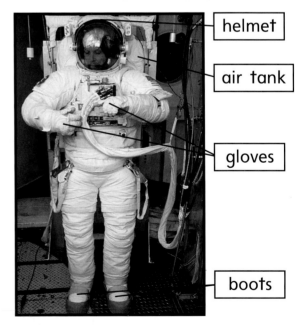

helmet

air tank

gloves

boots